Lift Bridge Publishing
info@liftbridgepublishing.com
www.lbpub.com
Lift Bridge Publishing:
Tel: (888) 774-9917

Printed in the United States of America

Publisher's Cataloging-in-Publication data

Watkins, Wes.

ISBN 9781637905197

Becoming a father was a job I was ready for.
Speaking into your life daily is a responsibility
I gladly take on.
Being there for you always is something I will
always do.
Telling you I love you everyday and hearing
you say it back puts the biggest smile on my
face.
When bad times arrive in my life, I can think
of your smiles and jokes and it makes me feel
better.
You can always count on me to be there for
you no matter what.
Nothing can separate us or take away the love
I have for you.

-Wes Watkins

Fathers are supportive and affectionate to their kids.
Children benefit from the involvement of a father.
Dads help children communicate, grow, and strengthen their minds and bodies.
A father is always helping to push and support their kids in sports or anything else a kid wants to do.
Fathers are always there showing love and support no matter what.
We need our fathers.

-Demauri Watkins

You are strong, confident, courageous and cool.
Beautiful, loving, and handsome too.

You're smart and bold with a very dope style.
I wrote this book for you, my special black child.

Did you know I love you very much?
I love your natural hair and shea butter skin.
Daddy loves your happy touch.

You make me smile.
I'm so proud of you.
You are my strong black Queen and King,
And no one can stop you.

Because of you, my life is great.
Our bond is something I could never escape.

The joy and laughter you bring to my heart
Will keep us connected and never apart.

I will protect you always
From this crazy world,
My handsome son and beautiful girl.

Show you right from wrong and the way to go.
I love when we watch our funny shows.

Daughter, you can talk to me about anything.
Daddy will always listen.
I'll help you solve your problems,
No matter what you mention.

Son, always look a man in his eye
When you shake his hand.

Always treat people with respect.
You will get the same in return when you become a man.

The fun times we have can never be replaced.
I love making memories with you
While running around outside in the open space.

I thank God everyday
For blessing me with you.

You make my heart smile and dance
Every time I look at you.

Becoming a dad has been my greatest joy.
I love spending time with you
And playing toys.

As a strong black father it's my job to protect.
I'll never neglect or allow anyone to disrespect
The beautiful child that I know you are.

I raised you to be proud of your skin and your hair.
I taught you different lessons like life isn't fair.
I taught you respect and not to be rude,
But make sure they respect you just as you do.

When you were created, God placed us together.
He knew I needed you and that we would be good together.
The times you cried He knew I'd be there
Just to hold you and show you I care.

Daddy will teach you how to watch out for the fake.
I will always motivate and push you to be great.

Your energy is something that the world needs.
Just be yourself and live your life free.

Never stop dreaming.
Keep reaching for the stars.
You're going to be great in life.
I know that you will go far.

You give me purpose in life,
And you make me smile.
You're my heartbeat.
I'm so glad you're my child.

CPSIA information can be obtained
at www.ICGtesting.com
Printed in the USA
BVRC090207031021
617853BV000022B/247